AF271053

▶ FEAR NOT! ◀
BE OUTRAGEOUSLY COURAGEOUS
Student Journal

Written by Randy Petersen

Editor: Stan Campbell
Cover Design: Scott Rattray
Cover Illustration: Robert Bergin
Text Design: Cheryl Blum, Helen Lannis
Adventure Series Editor: Marian Oliver
Editorial Coordinator: Mitchell Vander Vorst

The Chapel Ministries is a nonprofit, nondenominational Christian outreach dedicated to fostering renewal among Christians and their churches. The quarter-hour *Chapel of the Air* radio broadcast (Monday-Saturday) and the half-hour *You Need to Know* television program (Monday-Friday) are aired across the U.S. and Canada. The "Chapel" has a growing ministry to churches, including regional pastors' conferences and the annual 50-Day Spiritual Adventure and 4-Week Worship Celebration. Since the 50-Day Adventure began in 1980, more than 2.7 million believers have participated.

Printed in the United States of America.

ISBN 1-879050-48-X

INTRODUCTION

I'm noticing a difference in movie heroes. For decades we've had the Clint Eastwood types, staring down the barrel of a gun, saying through clinched teeth, "Go ahead. Make my day."

But there's a new breed of hero. I just saw Keanu Reeves as a classic action hero with one big difference: *He was terrified.* You can see fear in the eyes of any number of characters played by this new class of stars—Denzel Washington, Johnny Depp, Winona Ryder, and many others. The characters of this new breed are learning to take action in spite of their fears.

I don't base my life on Hollywood, and neither should you, but I think this trend suggests that (1) Even tough people feel afraid; (2) It's okay to express fear; and (3) If we face down our fears, we can gain the upper hand.

The Bible confirms these three points. God's people face all sorts of frightful things in the pages of Scripture: wars, floods, famines, personal conflicts, evil leaders, slavery, imprisonment, death threats, and lots more. God does not tell us to ignore such problems, but he does assure us that *he is with us.* "For God did not give us a spirit of timidity," the Apostle Paul wrote to a young minister, "but a spirit of power, of love and of self-discipline" (2 Timothy 1:7).

And that's what this 50-Day Spiritual Adventure is all about—leaving behind our timidity (and fear) and trying some new ways to serve God. If we are ruled by fear, life is never much of an adventure. But with our Lord giving us courage each day of this Adventure, we can face our fears square in the eye and say, "Go ahead, Lord, make my day."

During this Adventure, we'll focus on eight fears we need to face down.

Week 1: Face down the fear of a society that's breaking down.

Week 2: Face down the fear of living insignificant lives.

Week 3: Face down the fear of rejection.

Week 4: Face down the fear of the big "F" (failure).

Week 5: Face down the unhealthy fear of God.

Week 6: Face down the fear of sickness, aging, and death.

Week 7: Face down the fear of threats to our families.

Week 8: Face down the fear of the rise of evil.

1. Think about your fears. Think about what changes you'd like to see take place in your life through this Adventure.

2. Ask God to help you in a special way during the next seven weeks. Ask him what changes *he'd* like to see in your life through this Adventure.

3. Commit yourself to being serious about this Adventure. If you give it some time and attention, there's a great payoff. Check it out for a few days, and then try to make a solid commitment to the program before the first week is out.

4. Be Honest with yourself, and with God, as you answer the questions in this journal. An idea: If you're afraid someone might read your journal, use code words for delicate subjects—but don't avoid dealing with sensitive issues.

5. Relax. If you miss a day, don't drive yourself crazy trying to make up for lost time. Just resume the journal on the current day.

6. Connect with others. Try doing this Adventure with a few friends, your family, or your youth group. You can hold each other accountable and provide new ideas for each other.

7. Prepare yourself by reading the introductory material on pages 5–13. See what's coming up. During the Adventure you'll be taking five action steps. Some are pretty basic and familiar—like Scripture reading and prayer. Others involve more preparation. But don't worry! You'll get reminders every day to help you keep on track. The "Warm-up Days," Friday and Saturday before Day 1, are optional, but they can get you off to a good start.

The top of each page in this journal has a blank for the date. Go right now and get a calendar. Write the dates, in order, on all the pages. That way, if you miss a few days, it will be easier for you to find your spot and jump back in. (Notice that the seventh week is actually weeks 7 and 8. Week 8 starts on Thursday, Day 46.)

8. Expect to grow. God can move in mighty ways when his people try new things and let the Holy Spirit work through them in bold new ways. It can happen to you.

Face the Unknown with Confidence in the Known

This Adventure will challenge you to memorize one Bible verse each week. Here's why:

In every horror film ever made, the young heroine hears a noise in the distance and walks toward it—usually through a graveyard. (I have never figured out why she walks *toward* the sound. Why doesn't she run away?)

Anyway, she's walking through this creepy place, and it's dark, and the background music gets really eerie and . . . she starts to sing. Nothing fancy, just any little tune to comfort her. Or she repeats words of assurance she heard from some wise person in the movie—*anything* to give her courage until Freddy or Jason or some other maniac suddenly leaps in front of her.

What do you do in your life to keep yourself going? How do you get through the frightening moments? I would suggest repeating some wise words of assurance (or singing them). As you tiptoe through the dark places in your life, remember the comforting words of Scripture. Recite them to yourself, put them to music—they will help you keep going.

In Scripture, God regularly reminds his people that he is always there for them. "Do not be afraid," is one of his favorite phrases. As the psalmist wrote in one familiar verse, "Even though I walk through the valley of the shadow of death, I will fear no evil, for you [God] are with me" (Psalm 23:4).

But how can you recall God's words of comfort if you don't know them? That's why this action step has been included. You'll have God's words in your head, ready to use whenever you hear a strange sound in the distance and, inexplicably, move toward it.

For each day of this Adventure, there's an assigned Scripture passage in this journal. Read it and answer the study questions, which are designed to help you figure out how the scripture relates to your life. Once a week you'll be asked to memorize a verse. Consider having a friend check you on the verse during the week, and throughout the 50-Day Adventure. Track your progress using the checklist on the next page (p. 6). You'll have an opportunity to use these verses daily as a part of the Facing Down Our Fears Prayer (Action Step 2).

SCRIPTURE MEMORY PASSAGES

Week 1: The Fear of a Society That's Breaking Down

- [ ] John 16:33

Week 2: The Fear of Living Insignificant Lives

- [ ] Romans 8:16

Week 3: The Fear of Rejection

- [ ] Hebrews 13:6

Week 4: The Fear of the Big "F" (Failure)

- [ ] Psalm 37:23–24

Week 5: The Unhealthy Fear of God

- [ ] Psalm 103:13

Week 6: The Fear of Sickness, Aging, and Death

- [ ] Psalm 23:4

Week 7: The Fear of Threats to Our Families

- [ ] Psalm 103:17

Week 8: The Fear of the Rise of Evil

- [ ] 2 Thessalonians 3:3

Check the box next to the weekly scripture when you have memorized it.

Personalize the "Facing Down Our Fears Prayer"

What are you most afraid of? A terrorist attack or tomorrow's exam? Being mugged on a city street or being embarrassed by your friends? The national debt or your personal finances?

We fear all sorts of threatening events, big and little, faraway and nearby. Some people may think our fears are silly, but that doesn't help. We're still afraid. And fear can paralyze us, keeping us from trying new things, stunting our growth.

When we hand over our fears to God, he does not make fun of us. He merely says, "Let me take care of that. Relax, I'm here for you." That makes a *big* difference.

Some people will still be the victims of terrorist attacks, and others will still fail exams, but God gives us some perspective during such times. He cradles us firmly in his hands, and provides confidence. We'll still feel afraid from time to time, but when we know God is there, we can get past our fears and move ahead with life.

Every day, pray the Facing Down Our Fears Prayer. You don't have to say it word for word. Use the model on the following page (p. 8) as a guide, and pray from your heart.

Notice that you'll have to fill in a few things. First, you'll need to identify something you're fearful about. This may change during the course of the Adventure. One day it may be an escaped criminal in your neighborhood, the next day, college tuition.

Then plug in the memory verse you're learning for the week. "Wait," you might say. "Why are we quoting Scripture to God? Didn't he give us all of these verses to begin with?" Yes, but you should think of this prayer (any prayer, really) as a *dialogue.* God talks to you through these words of Scripture—so take the time to really listen for his message.

PRAYER

· · · · · · · · ·

LORD,

I know that when I feel AFRAID, you want to calm my heart.

Yet at this moment,

I'm **not** at peace about ________________________________.

The enemy wants me to be **consumed** by this **FEAR.**

But YOUR Word reminds me:
[fill in memory verse].

Thank you that as I face down my fears,
you are always with me.

Amen.

Be a Barnabas—EnCOURAGE Others

When I was in high school, we did our best to "cut down" each other. This had nothing to do with power tools or kitchen utensils—our weapons were words. We competed to see who could deliver the greatest insult. It was great fun to create good put-downs, but not so enjoyable to be on the receiving end.

As I look back, I see the damage we did to each other. Many of us had deep insecurities—we were afraid that we were too fat, or too skinny, or too short, or too dumb, or too loud, or too quiet, or had too many zits, or too few friends. When we tossed our "cuts" back and forth, we thought we were just fooling around, but many of us were deeply hurt and just too stubborn to show it.

It could have been very different. What if we had competed to see who could deliver the best *compliment*? What if we tried just as hard to *encourage* each other? Instead of growing up filled with fears and self-doubts, we might have found the courage to do more with our lives.

In the Bible, a man named Barnabas went with Paul on his first missionary journey. A young guy named John Mark went along also, but he left the trip halfway through. (We aren't told why. Perhaps he grew homesick or maybe he was a bit scared of the people who opposed Paul's efforts to preach the gospel.) When they were planning their second trip, Paul refused to take John Mark along. I can imagine the "cuts" that might have been delivered—"He's a deserter! He couldn't take it! He had to run home to Mama!" (Paul was a good man but not perfect.)

Barnabas, whose name means "Encourager,"* wanted to give John Mark a second chance and even insisted on it. As a result, Barnabas and Paul split up. Imagine how Mark must have felt. He was still young and already a failure—until Barnabas stood up for him. Barnabas' encouragement put the *courage* back into him.

I know Bar-Nabas is literally "Son of Encouragement," but what does that mean? No one today uses "Son of" in that way. What it meant was that he was a "man of encouragement." Today we might call him "Mr. Encouragement."

Did it make a difference for John Mark? You bet! A few years later Paul specifically requested Mark's assistance, calling him "helpful to me in my ministry" (2 Timothy 4:11). And this is the same Mark who later wrote one of the four Gospels.

By offering encouragement instead of put-downs, we can provide each other with power to help fight our fears.

'SUP? *Who needs encouragement? Look around at your classmates, your family, the people at church. As you put yourself in their shoes, who seems to need encouragement right now? Jot down some of their names here as you think of them now and throughout the Adventure.*

____

____

____

____

____

How could *you* play Barnabas with these people? Could you give an encouraging phone call or drop them a nice note? Could you let them know you're praying for them, or even offer to wash their car or cut their grass?

At least three times during this Adventure, do something encouraging for someone who needs it. Circle the names above when you have been an encourager for someone (or use a highlighter).

MORE AND MORE STUDENTS ARE RELYING ON PRIVATE COACHING FIRMS TO HELP THEM SCORE HIGHER ON THE SATs.

Dare to Pull Off an Outrageously Courageous Act

It looks so easy on the commercials, doesn't it? People are hang gliding and bungee jumping as if they don't have a fear in the world. "Just do it!" they say. "Grab all the gusto you can get!"

Keep the gusto; I want my body in one piece, thank you.

Many of us are gripped by a fear of failure. We don't try new things in life because we're afraid we won't succeed, we'll make fools of ourselves, or we'll get hurt. We learn to play it safe. Sometimes we even convince ourselves it's the "spiritual" thing to do.

But when you take a close look at the Bible, you find a lot of risk-takers, people who stepped out in faith and tried some outrageous things, in God's power, for God's glory.

We want to get past the fear of failure during this Adventure. Do something outrageous for God. Or at least try to. There is no disgrace in trying something and failing. The Lord will be very pleased with your efforts.

At least one time during this Adventure do an OUTRA-GEOUSLY COURAGEOUS ACT on behalf of the Lord—something you wouldn't normally dare to do. Here's some ideas:

 Talk to a friend about Christ

 Invite someone to your youth group

 Befriend the "loser" at school

 Introduce yourself to some of your neighbors

 Volunteer to work with an inner-city ministry

 Sign up for a short-term mission

 Unleash a hidden talent in church (singing, speaking, acting, etc.)

We don't just want you to do something *good*. We want you to do something *hard*. Confront your own fear of failure by trying something outrageously courageous. Come up with some ideas of your own and run them by your youth leader to see what he or she thinks of them.

Questions in this journal during the days and on pages 48–49 will help you prepare for your outrageously courageous act by helping you identify and analyze your fears, by asking God for ideas and power to carry them out. These questions will also help you evaluate your effort afterward.

Break Free from the Unhealthy Fear of God

The principal wants to see you in his office during second period. You begin thinking of all the bad things he might be nailing you for. That food-launching in the cafeteria was just applesauce. And the dissected crayfish in your biology teacher's lunch bag—no harm was done. What could it be?

You are sure that all your college plans are ruined and your diploma is history.

Principal Scourby invites you in and makes small talk. You've been such a good student *blah blah blah*, you've shown fine character *blah blah*, honor roll *blah blah blah*, and how are your folks? *Why does he bother trying to be friendly? Why doesn't he just let the guillotine fall?*

At this point, you have what we might call an "unhealthy fear" of the principal. He's trying to be a nice guy, but you sit there quaking like the San Andreas Fault. If you'd only listen, you'd know that the principal is bestowing upon you the annual scholarship of the local Ladies Convenience Store Auxiliary—all expenses paid to the institution of your choice.

Are you ready for the spiritual application of this scenario? Here it goes: We treat God like Principal Scourby. We cower in fear when we should be enjoying a friendly relationship with him. He wants to know us, to love us, to shower us with blessings, but we straight-arm him or run away. We need to learn to accept his love. We must maintain a healthy respect, sure, but no more quaking.

◄‥‥‥‥‥ 'SUP?: *Get hold of a copy of that phenomenal new book* How to Fear God without Being Afraid of Him *by David New and me, Randy Petersen. Read two chapters a week for the first four weeks and deal with the discussion/reflection questions. It's a short book, a quick read. (The book is also available on cassette.)*

After reading the book, schedule a Discussion Time. If your family or youth group is doing the Adventure, you may want to talk through the "fearing God" issue with them. Or gather a couple of friends at a local pizza place to talk this over. You can use the questions during Week 5 or the discussion/reflection questions in *How to Fear God Without Being Afraid of Him* to help guide your discussion.

While you are just getting into the Adventure, you can refer back to this list for a brief review of the action steps and how often you're to do each one. (For a more complete description of the action steps, see pp. 5–12.) Don't worry about keeping it all in your head. This journal will also give you daily reminders to guide you through the Adventure.

DAILY

Action Step 1: *Face the Unknown with Confidence in the Known*

Read the Bible passage for each day and answer the questions in the journal. Work throughout the Adventure to memorize the short Scripture memory passages. Store these words in your heart.

Action Step 2: *Personalize the "Facing Down Our Fears Prayer"*

Pray the Facing Down Our Fears Prayer using the words on page 8 as a guide.

WEEKLY

Action Step 5: *Break Free from the Unhealthy Fear of God*

Weeks 1–4: Read two chapters each week in *How to Fear God Without Being Afraid of Him*. Then, before the Adventure is over, plan a Discussion Time with family or friends to talk about what you've learned through the book.

THREE TIMES DURING THE ADVENTURE

Action Step 3: *Be a Barnabas—EnCOURAGE Others*

Look for people you may be able to encourage. Three times during the Adventure, show support for someone through a kind deed or word.

ONCE DURING THE ADVENTURE

Action Step 4: *Dare to Pull Off an Outrageously Courageous Act*

Seeking God's guidance and strength, do something courageous on behalf of the Lord—something you normally wouldn't dare to do. Questions on pages 48–49 will help you prepare for and evaluate your effort.

Read Philippians 4:4–9.

1. In verses 6–7, we find something we're not supposed to do, something we *are* supposed to do, and a result. What are these do's and don'ts?

The thing not to do? _______________________________

The thing to do? _______________________________

The result? _______________________________

2. English lesson: What's the main verb in verse 7? What's the subject of that verb? Why do you think Paul chose these words?

Verb: _______________________________

Subject: _______________________________

____

3. According to these verses, which of the following would be good strategies to use in facing fearful situations? (Check all that apply.)

- [ ] Worrying
- [ ] Being gentle
- [ ] Going to the beach
- [ ] Praying
- [ ] Rejoicing
- [ ] Worrying and fretting
- [ ] Worrying so much you get ulcers
- [ ] Asking God to improve the situation
- [ ] Worrying a lot
- [ ] Picking a fight with someone, just to let off steam
- [ ] Focusing on good things in the situation
- [ ] Complaining to everyone who will listen
- [ ] Complaining to people who won't listen
- [ ] Following the example of a respected Christian

4. Action Step 2 in this Adventure is a daily prayer. After reading today's verses, how do you think praying might help you deal with the fears in your life?

____

- [ ] I have read the introduction material in this journal including the explanation of the five action steps (see pp. 3–13).
- [ ] I have read the Facing Down Our Fears Prayer on page 8.

Read Luke 4:1–13.

1. Why do you think Jesus fasted for 40 days?

____

____

2. Jesus' three responses to the devil's temptations all had something in common. What was it?

☐ Crying ☐ Quoting Scripture

☐ Pretending to give in, but not really doing so

☐ Engaging in theological discussion

☐ Calling him names ☐ Zapping him with lightning

3. How did the devil respond to Jesus' strategy?

____

____

4. Did you notice that the devil quoted Scripture himself? What do you think this indicates about the way we use Scripture?

____

____

5. One of the key steps in this Adventure is daily reading of God's Word. How do you think this might help you deal with fears?

____

____

☐ I have read the introduction material in this journal including the explanation of the five action steps (see pp. 3–13).

☐ I have read the material on facing down the fear of a society that's breaking down on pages 16–17, which introduces this next week's Adventure theme.

☐ I have started memorizing John 16:33.

☐ I have begun praying the Facing Down Our Fears Prayer (see p. 8).

When Everything Falls Apart

a kid got shot the other day, standing on the corner, minding his own business. A car full of other kids hurtled down the street and, well, this kid was wearing the wrong colors. *Bang, bang*, you're dead. A drive-by, they call it.

What's this world coming to?

In science class you learn about ozone depletion, global warming, ultraviolet rays, and the shrinking rain forests. You may try to recycle your pop cans, but what good does that really do? Will there be any world left for you to enjoy as an adult? Or is the whole environment spinning out of control?

Kimba just learned that her parents are splitting up. It used to be so nice at home, but then everyone just started drifting away from each other. She saw it coming, but there was nothing she could do. Now her parents will be like many other parents—divorced.

Is there any way we can slam on the brakes to keep the world from going by so fast? Can we just sit down and talk about where we're going? Can we ever get back to when things made a little more sense?

The forces of our society are strong. It's like everyone is sliding down this steep hill. Who knows what will be found at the bottom? The world can be a terrifying place. Society seems to be getting more violent, more selfish, and more corrupt with each passing day. What does the future hold? Will there even *be* a future?

If you are afraid about these things, you have good reason to be. It means your eyes are open, and you see what's going on. But there's good news in the middle of all this gloom. *If you know God, you don't have to be afraid, because God is still in control.*

Jesus said it succinctly in our memory verse for this week:

"In this world you will have trouble. But take heart! I have overcome the world" (John 16:33).

The New Testament speaks often of "the world" operating by a system that ignores or rejects God. God loves the people in the world and longs to redeem them, but the *system* rebels against him.

So it should come as no surprise that we see violence in our present world-system. People are ignoring God's respect for human life. It only makes sense that people would destroy the environment, since they fail to appreciate God as Creator. *Of course* our society makes it hard for families to stay together, since the self-sacrificing love of Jesus Christ is ignored.

And as we take a minority stand for Christ and his ways, we can expect to make some enemies. We are going against "the system."

"In this world," Jesus warns us, "you will have trouble." But thankfully the verse does not end there. Jesus has beat the system. "I have overcome the world."

Through his sacrificial death, Jesus has won the redemption of those who trust him. And some day he will emerge as the ruler of all he has made. The score may be tilted against us now, but we are on the winning team.

So what can we do to face down the fear of a society that's breaking down?

KEEP YOUR FOCUS ON JESUS AND HIS ULTIMATE TRIUMPH.

Have you had driver's ed. yet? One safe-driving tip I learned was "aim high in steering." If you look down at the road right in front of you, you'll drift right or left, just trying to keep the car on the road. But if you focus higher, on the horizon, your steering will be smooth and safe.

In the same way, if we focus on the bad events around us, we can quickly get off track. But if we remember the long-range victory of Jesus and focus on him, it puts everything else into perspective.

Beat the system.

See yourself as a revolutionary, daring to live Jesus' way in a world that doesn't approve. Fight fear with fire, the fire of the Holy Spirit's presence in your life. Be aware of all the subtle ways "the system" tries to control you—through TV, music, movies, peer pressure—and make it a point to filter such influences through God's Word.

CAUTION: Remember that Jesus' way involves love and joy as much as righteousness. Don't be holier-than-thou and don't get cynical.

LEND A HAND.

Look for opportunities to help others. If your friends are overcome by fear, help them to see Jesus more clearly. If they start getting involved in some bad behavior, give them the encouragement they need to stop.

Remember that many people who don't know Jesus at all are just as frustrated with violence and ignorance as you are. Philippians 2:12–16 talks about Christians who "shine like stars" in the middle of a similar society.

These believers "hold out the word of life." Maybe you can tell these people that there is a better way, in Jesus. Shine like a star.

MEMORY VERSE

John 16:33
I have told you these things, so that in me you may have peace. In this world you will have trouble. But take heart! I have overcome the world.

We're printing the memory verse each week from the New International Version, but feel free to learn it from any version you like.

Jesus was speaking to his disciples in the Upper Room, the night before his crucifixion. His words in John 16:33 may have been spoken during the Last Supper. Jesus had just promised to send the Counselor, the Holy Spirit, to live within the disciples.

1. Check off any of the following times when you think you might need to remember this verse:

☐ When people make fun of your faith

    ☐ When your friends seem apathetic about Christ

☐ When you're disgusted by the evil in the world

    ☐ When you're worried about violence in your community

☐ When you're concerned about the future of the world

    ☐ When you're in trouble so deep you don't know what to do

☐ When there's a divorce in the family

    ☐ When there's a death or illness of a close friend or relative

☐ Other ____

    ☐ ____

2. Quickly skim chapters 13–16. What were "these things" that Jesus had told the disciples?

____

____

3. Why was he telling them these things?

____

____

4. What kind of trouble have you had recently? Was this what Jesus was talking about?

____

____

5. How has Jesus overcome the world?

____

____

6. How does that make you feel?

____

____

7. How might people tell from *you* that Jesus has overcome the world? (Check all that apply.)

☐ You try to live by Jesus' values, not the world's

☐ You patiently endure teasing or hostility when people oppose your faith

☐ You stay as far away from unbelievers as possible

☐ You make sure to talk with Jesus in prayer regularly

☐ You don't go ballistic when you hear bad world news

☐ You wear T-shirts with Christian messages

☐ You sell your baseball-card collection to support world missions

☐ Other _______________________________________

☐ _______________________________________

☐ I have read the introductory material on pages 3–13.

☐ I have read the material on facing down the fear of a society that's breaking down on pages 16–17, which introduces this week's Adventure theme.

☐ I have begun praying the Facing Down Our Fears Prayer (see p. 8).

☐ I am memorizing John 16:33.

☐ I have started to read chapters 1–2 of *How to Fear God Without Being Afraid of Him.*

Read Psalm 112.

1. According to this psalm, what makes a person happy (blessed)?

____

____

2. How does the person in this psalm react to "bad news" (verse 7)? Why?

____

____

3. Which of the following areas are you most concerned about? Rank them in order of 1 to 10 (10 being the most concerned).

☐ The future of the world environment

   ☐ The economic future of the nation

      ☐ The moral decline of the nation

☐ Your family's health and well-being

   ☐ Your personal health

      ☐ Your education

☐ Your reputation with others

   ☐ Whether you will get into a high-paying career

      ☐ Whether the right person will fall in love with you

☐ Whether the San Jose Sharks will ever win the Stanley Cup

4. How can you keep your heart "steadfast" when you're facing all of these fears and others that are even worse?

____

____

☐ I have read the introductory material on pages 3–13.

☐ I have read the material on facing down the fear of a society that's breaking down on pages 16–17.

   ☐ I have prayed today using the Facing Down Our Fears Prayer (see p. 8).

   ☐ I am memorizing John 16:33.

   ☐ I have started to read chapters 1–2 of *How to Fear God Without Being Afraid of Him.*

Read Deuteronomy 34:5–Joshua 1:9.

oses had led the Israelites out of Egypt and to the border of the Promised Land. He was the only leader the nation had ever had. Now Joshua had to replace him.

1. If you had been Joshua, what three words might describe your state of mind at this point?

1. _Anxiety_
2. _Fear_
3. _Excited_

2. What would you say to the people? Write the first 25 words of Joshua's inaugural speech—as if *you* were giving it.

The Lord has spoken to me. He's commanded me to be your leader — were moving out

3. God lists several things Joshua *should* do and should *not* do. What are they?

Should Do:
Be courageous
Trust and
remember

Should Not Do:
Look left or right

Circle or highlight the guidelines above that are still appropriate for our lives today.

4. In the last verse of this passage, what reason does God give for *not* being terrified?

5. If you really believed this promise (and remembered it more often), what changes would you expect in your life?

☐ I have prayed today using the Facing Down Our Fears Prayer (see p. 8).

☐ I am memorizing John 16:33.

☐ I have started to read chapters 1–2 of *How to Fear God Without Being Afraid of Him.*

Read 2 Chronicles 20:1–17.

1. What headline would you write about this passage for the *Jerusalem News*? (Remember: The battle hadn't taken place yet.)

____

____

2. This passage is full of "sound bites"—mini-memory verses that can help you keep a clear perspective on your fears. Find at least three and jot them down here. (See especially verses 12, 15, and 17.)

1. _______________________________________

2. _______________________________________

3. _______________________________________

3. Who have you "done battle with" lately? (Check all that apply.)

- ☐ Parents
- ☐ "The System"
- ☐ Brother(s) or sister(s)
- ☐ Best friend
- ☐ Other _______________

- ☐ Teachers
- ☐ Boss or coworkers
- ☐ Boyfriend or girlfriend
- ☐ Youth leader

- ☐ Classmates
- ☐ Friends at church
- ☐ Ex-friends at church
- ☐ Your pet

4. Of all the battles you marked, in which cases were you in the right? Go back through the ones you checked and circle any of them where you think God would want to help you "win." Then go through them one more time and mark the ones where you may never *win*, but that God can help you *endure*.

5. What message does this passage contain for all of your "battles"?

____

____

- ☐ I have prayed today using the Facing Down Our Fears Prayer (see p. 8).
- ☐ I am memorizing John 16:33.
- ☐ I am reading chapters 1–2 of *How to Fear God Without Being Afraid of Him.*

Read Psalm 11.

We don't know exactly what was happening in David's life at this time, but it's clear that "the righteous" were facing hard times because of "the wicked." Some people were encouraging David to run away from his problems, but he knew that he could find security in the Lord.

1. Is there a place where you almost always feel safe? If so, where?

____

2. In what way is God like a "refuge," similar to your safe place?

____

3. How do people you know "flee" from their problems?

____

4. In David's day some people apparently felt that the "foundations" of society were "being destroyed" (verse 3). Some feel that way about today's society. How would you respond?

- [ ] Yes, it's as if an earthquake has shaken our foundation
- [ ] Yes, but it's not beyond repair
- [ ] Well, maybe a few bricks have fallen, but that's all
- [ ] No, the foundation's still looking good
- [ ] Not at all; in fact, great new additions are being built
- [ ] Other ___________________________________
- [ ] _______________________________________

5. How would you answer the question asked in verse 3? What *can* righteous people do when society is in turmoil?

____

- [ ] I have prayed today using the Facing Down Our Fears Prayer (see p. 8).
- [ ] I am memorizing John 16:33.
- [ ] I'm reading chapters 1–2 of *How to Fear God Without Being Afraid of Him.*

Read Philippians 2:12–16.

1. In this text the Apostle Paul draws a sharp distinction between proper Christian behavior and the character of his "generation" (verse 15). What words and phrases does he use to describe what Christians *should* do?

____

2. What words and phrases are used for what Christians should *not* do?

____

3. What words does he use to describe his generation?

____

4. What words would you use to describe your generation?

____

5. In light of today's text, how should a Christian act in a generation like the one you have described above?

____

6. You might hold out food to a hungry person or hold out a life preserver to someone who is drowning. How can you "hold out the word of life" in your world? (Check the three best ways.)

- [ ] Hand out free Bibles in history class
- [ ] Hold up a "John 3:16" sign at the Chess Club meeting
- [ ] Give words of comfort to a hurting friend
- [ ] Wear a T-shirt printed with the entire text of the Book of Romans
- [ ] Let your science class know that you believe in a Creator
- [ ] Carry a sign that says, "Repent! The world will end after sixth period."
- [ ] Let others see the joy of Christ in you
- [ ] Tell your friends how wicked this world has become
- [ ] Other ____

- [ ] I have prayed today using the Facing Down Our Fears Prayer (see p. 8).
- [ ] I have memorized John 16:33 and recorded my progress on page 6.
- [ ] I've read chapters 1–2 of *How to Fear God Without Being Afraid of Him.*

Will It Matter That I Was?

"Tell me about something good you've done recently."

I was talking with my friend Christine, a college student, and I made this request, trying to make conversation. But she responded as if I were asking her to explain the theory of relativity. She couldn't think of anything.

"All right," I said. "Make it your whole life. Tell me about something good you've done during your lifetime."

She was still drawing a blank.

Unfortunately, many people feel this way. They don't see that they have ever done anything good. They fear that they will live and die as zeroes, not heroes.

Young people are especially prone to this fear of insignificance. Think about it. You grow up being told, "You're not old enough. You don't count." You go to high school and compete for the few positions of athletic and academic "stardom." But if you don't become the starting quarterback, the head cheerleader, the valedictorian, or the lead in the play, then you silently take your place with the rest of the nobodies.

Maybe you go to college, if you can afford it. But it's just another dog-eat-dog world. A few people shine; the rest muddle through. Maybe you'll get a job, if there are any jobs left for you. But will your job make any difference in the world, or will you just spend your life screwing the caps on tubes of toothpaste?

Every day we see people who have made it, and we dream of being like them. We see famous athletes playing their games, and we envy them. "That guy is really somebody," we say. "That actress must be really important." "If only I had my own alternative band, then people would pay attention to me." "If only I could be on TV, then I'd be somebody too."

Yeah, right.

Are you bothered by the fear of living an insignificant life? If so, how do you define significance?

Is it fame? Do you define significance by the number of people who know who you are? If so, do you really think Heather Locklear is making much of an impact on society? (Maybe she is, but not with her acting.)
Is it success? Is it **money**? Is it **political power**? Maybe some of these things do impact society, but don't fool yourself into thinking that these are definitions of "being somebody." You *are* somebody, because God made you somebody.

When we start worshiping fame and success, we can lose sight of the simple truth that God cares for every person. The Bible frequently reminds us that "There is no respect of persons with God"

(Romans 2:11, KJV). That doesn't mean he doesn't respect us. Rather, it means that he doesn't go along with all the levels we set up—this person being more important than that person. He cares for *all* of us, to the point of knowing how many hairs we have on our heads.

Who cares if your classmates think you're important? Who cares if your teachers pay attention to you? *God* is your biggest fan. He has the most time and effort invested in you. If you start with that assumption, you can relax a little. If God is for you, who can be against you?

As Christians, we have even more to be encouraged about. As our memory verse for the week says,

"The Spirit himself testifies with our spirit that we are God's children" (Romans 8:15-16).

Our significance comes from the fact that we're members of the greatest family on earth—God's family.

What should you do? *Do something significant . . . for God's kingdom.* Don't try to be famous; be real instead. Don't try to get rich; get righteous. Look for God's definition of significance. And here's one thing you'll learn: *Small things can be significant things.* When Jesus spoke of God's kingdom, he talked about tiny seeds and single pearls and pennies that drop through the floorboards. A mustard seed worth of faith can move a mountain. So don't aim to convert the whole world; show compassion to someone who needs it. That's significance!

In my conversation with Christine, I kept pressing her to think of something good she had done. Finally she said, "When I was in junior high, our group took some disadvantaged kids on a hayride. I helped organize it. That was pretty good, I guess."

She may never star in the Lollapalooza tour, but Christine has already lived a significant life. I bet you have too.

LOUISE WAS STARTING TO DROP SOME SUBTLE HINTS THAT SHE DIDN'T WANT TO SEE VERN ANYMORE.

MEMORY VERSE

Romans 8:16
The Spirit himself testifies with our spirit that we are God's children.

Romans 8:16 is the "official" memory verse for this week, but once you get that down, try to memorize verse 15 too. And, since Romans 8 is one of the greatest chapters in the Bible, try to read the whole thing.

Through the first seven chapters of Romans, Paul has been building a case—in this chapter he nails it down. God is doing a new thing with his people. The Law of the Old Testament was a way of showing us that, in order to be truly righteous, we must have God's power. We can't do it ourselves. But thanks to Jesus Christ and God's Spirit at work in us, we *can* have that power.

This new system, Paul says, is not based on fear but on *relationship.* A noble Roman household had two types of people: slaves and family members. Slaves obeyed the master out of fear, but children obeyed their father out of love. Thanks to Jesus, we need not consider ourselves God's slaves—afraid of his expectations for us. Rather, we become his children.

NOTE: The word *Abba* in verse 15 is an intimate term for father. We might translate it, "Daddy!"

1. Which of the following situations are you facing where Romans 8:15–16 can help give you peace of mind?

- [ ] God seems far away
- [ ] You don't understand what God is doing
- [ ] You've sinned and you're sorry
- [ ] Other people question your Christian commitment
- [ ] It seems impossible to please God
- [ ] Other ___________________________________
- [ ] ___________________________________

2. Do you know people you would describe as being "slaves to fear"? What are the consequences of having such fears in their lives?

____

____

3. How does God's Spirit let you know (testify with *your* spirit) that you are his child? (Check all that apply.)

☐ A small voice

    ☐ Assurance from other believers

☐ Skywriting

    ☐ The changes he's making in your life

☐ The words of Scripture

    ☐ A sense of peace even at frightening times

☐ A blinding light from heaven

    ☐ Secret codes on car license plates

☐ Other _______________________________

    ☐ _______________________________

4. How does it make you feel to know you're a child of God?

____

____

☐ I have read the material on facing down the fear of living insignificant lives on pages 25–26, which introduces this week's Adventure theme.

☐ I have prayed today using the Facing Down Our Fears Prayer (see p. 8).

☐ I have started memorizing Romans 8:16.

☐ I have started reading chapters 3–4 of *How to Fear God Without Being Afraid of Him.*

DAY 9

Read Esther 3:8-9; 4:1-17.

after a period of captivity in Persia, the Jews were released, and many of them returned to Judea. (See Nehemiah and Ezra.) Others, including Esther and her cousin Mordecai, remained and became part of that society. By winning a beauty contest, Esther had become a queen of the mighty King Xerxes. Haman was prime minister, serving under King Xerxes.

1. What was Haman planning to do?

____

2. How did Mordecai respond to Haman's plans?

____

3. Why was Esther afraid to approach the king?

____

4. What would you have done if you were Esther?

- [ ] Say, "Ha! I'm queen! What do I care?"
- [ ] Resign your queenship
- [ ] Storm into the king's throne room and tell him exactly what you think
- [ ] Have a nervous breakdown
- [ ] Other _______________________________

5. God put Esther where she was in order to do something very significant. What significant thing might God be preparing *you* to do?

____

The Book of Esther is as thrilling and dramatic as anything written by John Grisham or Stephen King. You may want to read the rest of it to see how the story turns out.

- [ ] I have prayed today using the Facing Down Our Fears Prayer (see p. 8).
- [ ] I have read the material on facing down the fear of living insignificant lives.
- [ ] I am memorizing Romans 8:16.
- [ ] I'm reading chapt. 3–4 of *How to Fear God Without Being Afraid of Him*.

DAY 10

Read Jeremiah 29:10–14.

The Babylonians had invaded Judah and taken most of the Israelites back to Babylon as captives. Jeremiah had predicted this, calling it God's judgment on the sin and idolatry of his people. Today's verses were directed to those Israelites in Babylonian exile.

1. What was God promising to do for his people?

____

2. How long would they be in captivity?

____

3. How do you think they felt during this time?

____

4. How do you think it helped to know that God had a purpose?

____

5. How do you usually respond to difficult circumstances?

- [ ] Cry a lot
- [ ] Punch somebody
- [ ] Pray a lot
- [ ] Blame God and stop praying
- [ ] Grit my teeth and work hard to overcome the difficulty
- [ ] Go to the beach
- [ ] Other _______________________

6. Have difficult circumstances ever made you wonder if there was any purpose to your life? Describe them. How did you get through those times?

____

- [ ] I have prayed the Facing Down Our Fears Prayer (see p. 8).
- [ ] I am memorizing Romans 8:16.
- [ ] I'm reading chapters 3–4 of *How to Fear God Without Being Afraid of Him.*

Read Galatians 2:17–21.

Paul has been talking about how Christ's crucifixion has provided us with a much better way to live than the previous rules-and-regulations system of law.

1. Focus on verse 20. How does Christ "live" *in* a believer?

____

____

2. Choose your favorite TV-commercial jingle and rephrase verse 20 to fit that tune. You will *never get it out of your head!* (Write your lyrics here.)

____

____

3. This week, your reading centers around the fear of being insignificant. That means we have to take a hard look at what significance really is. Take a look at the following list and rate, from 1 to 7, how significant *your friends* find these things (1 being most). Then in the second column, rate from A to G (A being most), how *you* determine significance.

Them	**You**	
☐	☐	How much money you have
☐	☐	How many friends you have
☐	☐	How many dates you get
☐	☐	How good a person you are
☐	☐	The grades you get
☐	☐	Your skill at sports
☐	☐	How you are serving Christ

4. Take some time now to talk with God about what *he* thinks is significant.

☐ I have prayed the Facing Down Our Fears Prayer (see p. 8).

☐ I am memorizing Romans 8:16.

☐ I'm reading chapt. 3–4 of *How to Fear God Without Being Afraid of Him.*

Read Micah 6:6–8.

1. According to this passage, which of the following do you think God would enjoy most?

☐ Your gift of a million dollars to the church and Christian organizations

☐ Your attendance at church every time the doors open, for 80 years

☐ Your consistent desire to learn from God how he wants you to act

2. Even Christians are frequently guilty of judging a person's significance by money or public abilities. But this passage reminds us of God's priorities. What specifically could you do in the next week to:

Act justly? ____

Love mercy? ____

Walk humbly with your God? ____________________________

We regularly hear about "significant" people on the news, but their significance is often based on worldly power or outlandish deeds. Be on the lookout this week for an example of someone who "acts justly, loves mercy, or walks humbly with God." You may see it on the news or in the paper—or it may be someone you see in real life. Record the facts here.

WHO? ____

WHAT? ____

WHERE? ____

WHEN? ____

WHY? ____

HOW? ____

☐ I have prayed today using the Facing Down Our Fears Prayer (see p. 8).

☐ I am memorizing Romans 8:16.

☐ I'm reading chapt. 3–4 of *How to Fear God Without Being Afraid of Him.*

Read Matthew 10:29–31.

The disciples were being sent out to tell people about the exciting new things God had planned for them. Jesus had just warned them that they would face opposition. Yet, while they might face *physical* punishment from the authorities, only God controlled eternal rewards and punishment.

1. Why does God care how many hairs you have?

____

2. If you were translating the Bible for a bald society living in a country with no birds, how would you translate these verses?

____

3. How do you think Jesus' words in today's verses made the disciples feel as they set off to preach?

____

4. Have you ever felt that your work for God was useless? Have you ever felt as if the opposition was too great? How can these verses help you?

____

____

☐ I have prayed today using the Facing Down Our Fears Prayer (see p. 8).

☐ I have memorized Romans 8:16 and recorded my progress on page 6.

☐ I've read chapters 3–4 of *How to Fear God Without Being Afraid of Him*.

In the Rejection Seat

Skip was the kid who was picked on from his first nervous day of seventh grade. He was the runt of the class—short, skinny, with a squeaky voice. He had a habit of doing ridiculous things, so we laughed at him.

I joined the others in mocking him. Why? I don't know. I'm not a cruel person, but there's something about junior high "mob mentality." I was afraid that if I stood up for Skip, the group would make fun of me too.

The passage through junior high into high school, and sometimes even into college, can be a tricky one. Competition is fierce. You want to make a name for yourself and claim your territory, but you probably have deep insecurities about what you look like and what you're capable of doing. At any moment, the group can turn on you. "Aha! Look at you, the pimple-faced moron! You're so ugly, my dog wouldn't go with you to the prom. You're so dumb, you studied all night for your blood test and still failed. You're so out of it, you think Pearl Jam is a toothpaste."

How do you avoid such criticism? You don't draw attention to yourself. And if the group is teasing someone else, you take a deep sigh of relief. At least it's not you. In fact, you better join right in.

The fear of rejection can stunt your growth. I'm serious. It can stunt emotional and spiritual growth because you become afraid to be yourself. You stop trying anything new, anything different, anything "you," because others might laugh. And that would hurt.

Another area where fear of rejection strikes is in matters of *romance*. "I like Maribeth. I really, really do. I've scribbled her name in my notebook a zillion times. But I don't dare talk to her, because she might shoot me down."

Fear of rejection keeps some Christian young people from sharing their faith with their friends. If word gets around that you're a Christian, you could get tossed out of the inner circle. So some Christian kids go undercover, doing the church thing on Sunday, but keeping their faith a secret during the week.

WILL'S NEW HABIT OF WEARING BOWLING SHOES TO SCHOOL WAS HAVING A NEGATIVE EFFECT ON HIS SOCIAL LIFE.

How do you face down the fear of rejection?

Understand that God accepts you. Once again, we need to expand our horizons. We need to lift our sights and discover what God thinks. What is God's opinion about you? He loves you. He knows you have sinned, and he *still* loves you. He longs for you to walk side by side with him in an exciting relationship.

Your acknowledgment that God accepts you should put everything else in perspective. As our memory verse this week says,

"The Lord is my helper; I will not be afraid. What can man do to me?" (Hebrews 13:6).

Even if we are rejected by others, we can deal with it, because God will see us through the rejection.

Accept yourself. Many people fear rejection from others because it confirms the rejection they already feel toward themselves. But when you see yourself as a beloved child of God, you should stop putting yourself down. You're told to "love your neighbor *as yourself*" (Matthew 22:39, italics added). We need to love God and others, but we also need an appropriate love for ourselves.

Does this mean we can do no wrong? Of course not! We still make mistakes. But God forgives us, and we should forgive ourselves.

Accept others. When people reject us, we tend to reject them back. Yet the Christian way is to *accept* people who reject us. It baffles the people around you. Answer insults with compliments. Encourage those who make fun of you. When others draw a circle to exclude you, draw your own circle around theirs to welcome them (and all the other excluded ones) to receive your love and acceptance.

One thing that always amazed me about Skip was that he never seemed to lash back in anger. He put up with our insults with silent dignity. By our junior year, he had become a class leader, heading up the debate team with his quick wit. By senior year, Skip had become a Christian and was instrumental in starting a Bible study group at school.

I'd like to say that it was my brilliant testimony that led Skip to Christ. It wasn't. It was his gracious behavior that taught me valuable lessons about rejection and acceptance that I'm now passing along to you. Maybe you can pass them along to someone else.

DAYS 14-15

MEMORY VERSE

Hebrews 13:6
So we say with confidence, "The Lord is my helper; I will not be afraid. What can man do to me?"

the author of Hebrews urges readers to "be content with what you have" (verse 5). God's presence should be the basis for our contentment. He has promised to be with us always. With the Lord as our "helper" (or "protector"), we don't need money or even popularity. We have him.

1. Check off the times below when you think this verse will be most important to you.

- ☐ When you want something you can't afford
- ☐ When people make fun of you for being a Christian
- ☐ When you worry about your future
- ☐ When you wonder whether God cares about you
- ☐ When everyone else seems richer and more popular
- ☐ Other ____

2. The author of Hebrews says to say this memory verse with "confidence." On a scale of 3 to 17, how confident are you about God's help? _____________

3. How has God helped or protected you in the past?

____

4. In the coming week we'll be emphasizing the need to encourage others. Who is one person who may need to hear the message of this verse?

____

5. How might you adapt this message specifically to that person? Use this space for a rough draft for what you might write or say to that person.

____

- ☐ I've read the material on facing down the fear of rejection on pages 34–35, which introduces this week's Adventure theme.
- ☐ I've prayed the Facing Down Our Fears Prayer (see p. 8).
- ☐ I've started memorizing Hebrews 13:6.
- ☐ I've started reading chapt. 5–6 of *How to Fear God Without Being Afraid of Him.*

Read Acts 9:19b–28.

Saul was an aggressive persecutor of Christians shortly after Jesus died and rose again. But on a trip to arrest Christians in Damascus, Jesus appeared to him, and Saul converted to Christianity. Later, he became the church's greatest missionary, using the name Paul.

1. When the Jews who opposed Christianity heard Saul preaching the Christian message in Damascus, how do you think they felt?

____

____

2. When Saul tried to see Jesus' disciples in Jerusalem, how do you think the disciples felt?

____

____

3. How do you think Saul felt after first being rejected by the disciples?

____

____

4. What was Barnabas' reaction to the disciples' rejection of Saul? What do you think made him support Saul?

____

____

5. You may know someone who has done bad things in the past, but now is sorry about his or her previous actions. How could you be a "Barnabas" (encourager) for this person? What might you write or say to that person?

____

____

☐ I have read the material on facing down the fear of rejection on pages 34–35, which introduces this week's Adventure theme.

☐ I've prayed today using the Facing Down Our Fears Prayer (see p. 8).

☐ I am memorizing Hebrews 13:6.

☐ I'm reading chapt. 5–6 of *How to Fear God Without Being Afraid of Him*.

☐ I am thinking of people to be a Barnabas for (see pp. 9–10).

Read Proverbs 12:25.

1. How would you describe an "anxious heart"?

____

2. Do you know people who are "weighed down" by an "anxious heart"? How would you describe their lives?

____

____

3. According to this verse, what difference could you make in the lives of such people?

____

____

4. When was the last time someone cheered you up with a kind word? What did that person say? What difference did it make to you?

____

____

barney the Dinosaur is still despondent because he didn't get the role of Dino in last summer's *Flintstones* movie. What could you say to cheer him up?

____

____

☐ I have prayed today using the Facing Down Our Fears Prayer (see p. 8).

☐ I am memorizing Hebrews 13:6.

☐ I'm reading chapt. 5–6 of *How to Fear God Without Being Afraid of Him.*

☐ I am thinking of people to be a Barnabas for (see pp. 9–10).

Read Psalm 27.

1. Do you know someone who needs a lot of encouragement right now? What are some phrases from this psalm that this person might need to hear?

____

____

____

2. In your judgment, on a scale of 1 to 10 (10 being the most), how important does the psalmist consider his relationship with others? ______ On the same scale, how important does he consider his relationship with God? ______

3. Verses 9–10 suggest that the psalmist even felt rejected by God. Sometimes people go through times like this; maybe you have, too. If you were in that frame of mind, what could you hear that might help?

____

____

____

he crew of "Star Trek: The Next Generation" is understandably depressed about having their TV show canceled, and they're not quite sure yet about movie possibilities. How could Counselor Troi try to comfort them?

____

____

☐ I have prayed today using the Facing Down Our Fears Prayer (see p. 8).

☐ I am memorizing Hebrews 13:6.

☐ I'm reading chapt. 5–6 of *How to Fear God Without Being Afraid of Him*.

☐ I have decided on someone to be a Barnabas for and have noted that on page 10.

►DAY 19◄

Read 2 Corinthians 1:3–4.

1. What are the four words used most often in these two verses?

    1. ___________________________

    2. ___________________________

    3. ___________________________

    4. ___________________________

2. How have you been comforted by God?

____

____

____

3. How does his comfort help you comfort others?

____

____

____

On "Home Improvement," if Tim were depressed because his new comfort machine broke down, what might Wilson (his wise neighbor) say to console him?

____

____

____

☐ I have prayed today using the Facing Down Our Fears Prayer (see p. 8).

☐ I am memorizing Hebrews 13:6.

☐ I'm reading chapt. 5–6 of *How to Fear God Without Being Afraid of Him.*

☐ I have decided on someone to be a Barnabas for and have noted that on page 10.

Read Psalm 56.

This psalm was written as David, who had been selected by God to be the *next* king of Israel, was on the run from Saul, the current king. He was also trying to contend with the traditional enemies of Israel, such as the nasty Philistines. (Hey, I'm tired of doing all this background stuff for you. Read 1 Samuel 21:10–22:2 for yourself to get some idea of all the stress in David's life at this time.)

1. Think of a situation that usually causes you to be afraid. What do you usually do in that situation?

____

____

2. What did David do when he was afraid? (Psalm 56:3)

____

____

3. Does verse 4 sound familiar? Why?

____

4. Think of the person or group or thing that you're most afraid of and insert that name in place of "mortal man" in verse 4. Say the new verse ten times today (a couple of times now and at various points throughout the day).

"What can _____________________ do to me?"
                (name)

☐ I have prayed today using the Facing Down Our Fears Prayer (see p. 8).

☐ I have memorized Hebrews 13:6 and recorded my progress on page 6.

☐ I've read chapt. 5–6 of *How to Fear God Without Being Afraid of Him*.

☐ I've been a Barnabas for someone and recorded my progress on page 10.

THE BIG "F"

I've never seen anyone so afraid. Linda was auditioning for the spring musical that I was directing. Her music teacher assured me she had a lovely voice, but I couldn't tell. Hardly any sound came out of her mouth. As Linda stood on stage, she wrung her hands rapidly. Her body was all twisted, shoulders and knees turned in. She looked right and left, up and down, but she never focused on anything. This girl was terrified.

What was she afraid of? She was afraid that she would do poorly, that she would not get the part she wanted, and that she would make a fool of herself. Guess what? She did poorly. She didn't get the part. She looked foolish. But it wasn't a lack of talent that made her fail—it was her fear.

It reminds me of Peter walking on the water. Jesus was out there walking the waves, so Peter, with his typical bluster, hopped out of the boat and walked toward Jesus. How far did he walk? We don't know. But suddenly he noticed how bad the conditions were—it was stormy, windy, and hey, there was only water beneath his feet. "He was afraid," the Bible says. What was he afraid of? Sinking! So what happened? He began to sink. It was a self-fulfilling fear. His fear of failure caused the failure.

Is the fear of failure holding you back? Is there some talent you think you might have, but you're afraid to find out? Do you long to try some project or shoot for some goal? Then go for it. Too much fear of failure will *guarantee* failure. As some witty person once said, "If you fail to try, you try to fail."

An even wiser saying comes from 2 Timothy 1:7: "God did not give us a spirit of timidity, but a spirit of power, of love and of self-discipline." Maybe we can learn some lessons from this verse about facing down the fear of failure.

Power. As Christians, we can step forward boldly in God's power. We're not trying to do something so *we* can brag about it, but so *God's* power can be shown through us. As our memory verse says this week:

"If the Lord delights in a man's way, he makes his steps firm; though he stumble, he will not fall, for the Lord upholds him with his hand" (Psalm 37:23-24).

We need to try to "delight" God as we use the abilities he has given us. And notice that he does not promise that we will never fail. We may stumble, but we will not be devastated. God will pick us up so we can try again.

Love. It's important to have a "fail-safe" group of friends around us as we try to work through our fear of failure. We need to be gentle with others who are attempting new things, and ask them to be gentle with us. During Linda's audition, if I had snapped, "That's pitiful! Get off the stage," she might never have tried out for anything again. Instead, I encouraged her, and the next year she tried out again and got a part.

Self-discipline. We need to work hard to develop the gifts we've been given. God does not guarantee us success in everything we do. We must discipline ourselves to excel in whatever we choose to try. With God-given abilities, solid preparation, and the courage we draw from our relationship with God, we can face down the fear of failure and move forward to achieve true success.

MEMORY VERSE

Psalm 37:23–24
If the Lord delights in a man's way, he makes his steps firm;
though he stumble, he will not fall, for the Lord upholds him
with his hand.

If you want to replace the word man's *with* person's *it may make it more mean-ingful for you.*

This entire psalm is a collection of sayings about wicked and righteous people. It almost sounds as if it belongs in the Book of Proverbs. It is attributed to David, who frequent-ly tussled with "evil men." Though he himself "stumbled" sometimes, he regularly tried to "commit his way to the Lord" (verse 5).

1. Check the times below when you think these verses will be most helpful.

☐ When you think that no one notices how good you're trying to be

☐ When the "bad kids" at school seem to have all the fun

☐ When you're the object of jokes because you're "too good"

☐ When you feel guilty about doing something wrong

☐ When you are tempted to do something wrong

☐ Other ________________________________

☐ ________________________________

2. What can you do to bring delight to God? (Check out verses 3–5)

____

____

____

3. As you read this psalm, what will be the final destiny of "the wicked"?

____

____

____

4. What can righteous people expect?

____

____

5. This week we'll be talking about the fear of failure. Certainly David had a few failures, most notably murder and adultery (see 2 Samuel 11). But David knew how to charge forward, to step out with courage. He repented of his sins and moved on. Are you afraid of failure? Specifically, what failure do you fear most?

____

____

6. Talk to God about your specific fears during this week. Ask for his perspective and his courage.

☐ I have read the material on facing down the fear of failure on pages 42–43, which introduces this week's Adventure theme.

☐ I have prayed today using the Facing Down Our Fears Prayer (see p. 8).

☐ I have started memorizing Psalm 37:23–24.

☐ I've started reading chapt. 7–8 of _How to Fear God Without Being Afraid of Him_.

☐ I've been a Barnabas for someone and recorded my progress on page 10.

☐ I am deciding on an outrageously courageous act (see p. 11).

WALT MESSES UP HIS RIGHT TURN SIGNAL ONCE AGAIN.

Read Matthew 14:22–33.

1. How did the disciples react when they saw Jesus walking on the water?

____

2. Why do you think Peter chose to step out of the boat?

____

3. After he got out of the boat, what made Peter afraid?

____

4. How do you think *you* would have acted in that situation?

- [ ] No way would I have ever stepped out of the boat
- [ ] I would have taken one step out and then climbed back into the boat
- [ ] I would have done exactly what Peter did
- [ ] I would have gone over the side, but I would've put on a life preserver
- [ ] I would have kept my eyes on Jesus the whole time
- [ ] I would have been partying back in Capernaum

5. Do you think Peter's actions were good or bad? Would it have been better for him to have stayed in the boat? Explain.

____

6. On a scale of 1 to 10, how afraid of failure do you think Peter was (10 being most afraid)? _______
On the same scale, how afraid of failure would you say *you* are? _______

- [ ] I have read the material on facing down the fear of failure on pages 42–43, which introduces this week's Adventure theme.
- [ ] I have prayed today using the Facing Down Our Fears Prayer (see p. 8).
- [ ] I am memorizing Psalm 37:23–24.
- [ ] I'm reading chapt. 7–8 of *How to Fear God Without Being Afraid of Him.*
- [ ] I've been a Barnabas for someone and recorded my progress (p.10).
- [ ] I am deciding on an outrageously courageous act (see p. 11).

Read 1 Samuel 17:1–50.

1. Why wasn't anyone willing to go out and fight Goliath?

____

2. How do you think Goliath felt as he challenged the Israelites day after day?

____

3. How do you think he felt when he saw David coming toward him?

____

4. Why did David go out to fight Goliath? What made him different from the other Israelites?

____

5. On a scale of 1 to 10, how "afraid of failure" do you think David was (10 being the most)? _______

6. You're a reporter for ESPN, doing a postbattle interview with David. Write your questions and how you might expect David to answer them below. (Your producer says you have to ask him something about the fear of failure.)

Question ___________________________________

Answer _____________________________________

Q. ____

A. ____

Q. ____

A. ____

☐ I have prayed today using the Facing Down Our Fears Prayer (see p. 8).

☐ I am memorizing Psalm 37:23–24.

☐ I am reading chapters 7–8 of *How to Fear God Without Being Afraid of Him*.

☐ I've been a Barnabas for someone and recorded my progress on page 10.

☐ I am deciding on an outrageously courageous act (see p. 11).

DARE TO PULL OFF AN OUTRAGEOUSLY COURAGEOUS ACT

Preparation and Evaluation

Part 1: Reread page 11

Part 2: Think
List some outrageously courageous acts that you believe God may be calling you to consider for this action step.

____

____

____

(If you need some help, consider these!)

- [ ] Talking to a friend about Christ
    - [ ] Inviting someone to youth group
- [ ] Befriending someone new at school
    - [ ] Introducing myself to some of my neighbors
- [ ] Volunteering to work with an inner-city ministry
    - [ ] Signing up for a short-term mission
- [ ] Using a hidden talent in church (singing, speaking, acting, etc.)
    - [ ] Volunteering to _______________________
- [ ] Other _______________________________
    - [ ] _______________________________

Part 3: Pray
Once you have thought of some ideas, pray! Talk to God about these ideas and ask that you will be open to doing what God wants you to do.

Part 4: Decide
What outrageously courageous act will you choose for this Adventure?

____

____

Part 5: Prepare

What about this scares you?

____

____

What preparations can you make that will help you be less afraid and more courageous?

____

____

Part 6: Do it!

Now that you have decided on what to do, begin planning. The first step is to go to God with your fear and ask him for courage. Then, choose the time you're going to do this act, and do it!

Part 7: Evaluate

Now that you have completed your outrageously courageous act, how did you do? Do you think you failed or succeeded?

____

____

Do you think God is pleased with your efforts? Are you pleased with your efforts?

____

____

What fears did you experience during this action step? Were you afraid of failing? What do you think of these fears now?

____

____

How might this action step help you to rely on God for courage and face down fears in the future?

____

____

Part 8: Can I do this again?

You may want to consider continuing this action step. Stay with your original outrageously courageous act, try again, or try some of your other ideas.

▶ DAY 25 ◀

Read 2 Timothy 1:3–7.

Timothy was a relatively young pastor (or church planter) in Ephesus. Previously he had been a companion on Paul's missionary travels. Now Paul writes to him from prison in what was probably his last epistle.

1. Record some of the difficulties you think Timothy was facing. (You'll need to look at some other verses.)

1 Timothy 4:11–15 _______________________________________

1 Timothy 5:21–23 _______________________________________

2. Why might Timothy have felt fearful (or timid) in his situation?

____

____

3. Paul mentions the "gift of God" that Timothy has (see 2 Timothy 1:6). This was probably some ability that related to church leadership. Why do you think Paul reminded Timothy of this?

____

____

4. What might *your* "gift of God" be? What special ability has God given you? If you don't know for sure, that's fine, but try to list some possibilities.

____

____

5. How might the awareness of your "giftedness" help you deal with a fear of failure?

____

____

☐ I have prayed today using the Facing Down Our Fears Prayer (see p. 8).

☐ I am memorizing Psalm 37:23–24.

☐ I am reading chapters 7–8 of *How to Fear God Without Being Afraid of Him*.

☐ I have decided on a second person to encourage and have noted that on page 10.

☐ I'm planning an outrageously courageous act (see pp. 11 and 48–49).

Read Hebrews 4:14–16.

1. According to this passage, how does Jesus view our weaknesses?

____

____

2. What does it say about the way we should approach God?

____

____

3. When we fail spiritually, what should we do?

☐ Just give up the faith entirely

    ☐ Try to punish ourselves by going without TV

☐ Do something good to show God we mean business, like helping an old man across the street—whether he wants to go or not!

    ☐ Sink into a deep depression

☐ Try to convince God that we really didn't do anything wrong

    ☐ Tell God we're sorry and ask for forgiveness

☐ Other ____

4. Some people are afraid to try anything new or different, for fear that they might fail. Do you know anyone like that? Based on this passage, what advice would you give to such a person?

____

____

☐ I have prayed today using the Facing Down Our Fears Prayer (see p. 8).

☐ I am memorizing Psalm 37:23–24.

☐ I'm reading chapt. 7–8 of *How to Fear God Without Being Afraid of Him.*

☐ I have decided on a second person to encourage and have noted that on page 10.

    ☐ I am planning an outrageously courageous act (see pp. 11 and 48–49).

DAY 27

Read 1 Chronicles 28:20.

david had wanted to build a temple for God, but God said the job belonged to David's son and successor, Solomon. Here, David gives Solomon advice about the project.

1. What if David were a coach, giving last-minute instructions to his star tennis player or gymnast, Solomon? How might that pep talk sound?

____

2. What discouraging circumstances might Solomon face in building the temple?

- [ ] A labor strike
- [ ] Price of cedar wood goes sky high after a forest fire in Lebanon
- [ ] Architects keep trying to put a steeple on it
- [ ] Stonecutters still using inferior Egyptian blades
- [ ] Local residents want to use the site for a ballpark
- [ ] Other _______________________________________
- [ ] _______________________________________

3. What reasons did David give for Solomon not to be discouraged?

____

4. What kind of "temple" are you building for God? You may be trying to develop your own abilities. Or you may be working on some project—sharing your faith with others or tutoring underprivileged kids. Do you ever get discouraged in the process? What could today's verse mean to you?

____

- [ ] I have prayed today using the Facing Down Our Fears Prayer (see p. 8).
- [ ] I have memorized Psalm 37:23–24 and recorded my progress on page 6.
- [ ] I've read chapt. 7–8 of *How to Fear God Without Being Afraid of Him*.
- [ ] I've been a Barnabas for two people and recorded my progress on page 10.
- [ ] I'm planning an outrageously courageous act (see pp. 11 and 48–49).

God Awful?

i was sick as a dog. I was sick as a very sick dog. "Why are you doing this to me, God?" I cried out. I confessed every sin I could think of. I probably made up some new ones. "Look, if you make me feel better, I will do anything. I will go to church 24 hours a day if you want. Just, please, make me feel better."

I was operating on the basic assumption that God was responsible for how I felt. If I felt lousy, he must be punishing me for something. If I were a better Christian, I would not be so sick.

I was wrong.

Many people have had similar experiences. Facing sickness, danger, or emotional pain, they fear that God must be getting back at them for something. Sometimes they try to buy him off with wild promises.

Some people live their entire lives with a negative image of God. In their eyes, God is little more than a harsh judge, eager to "catch them in the act" of sin and punish every little offense. They recognize that they can never live up to his holy standards. Some become fanatical about keeping his commands and continually scold themselves for their unworthiness. Others just stop trying. They still feel deeply guilty, but they know they can never live in a way that pleases God.

Does any of this ring a bell with you? Do you have an unhealthy fear of God? Do you constantly feel guilty? Do you worry about God punishing you? Do you find it difficult to forgive yourself for past sins? Does the thought of God strike such terror in your heart that you find it impossible to consider him your friend?

The problem with this point of view is that it's only half true. It shows a limited perspective of God. Yes, God is holy. Yes, God hates sin. Yes, *by ourselves* we can never measure up to his standards. But in Jesus Christ, we can.

God is a loving God and full of understanding. He has provided a way for us to know him. If we know Jesus, his Son, we are in his family. We can then experience a loving relationship with God the Father, in which we enjoy him, and he enjoys us. From time to time, we may still do wrong things, but God understands this tendency and stands ready to forgive us.

Our memory verse this week shatters the negative image of God as a harsh judge.

"As a father has compassion on his children, so the Lord has compassion on those who fear him, for he knows how we are formed, he remembers that we are dust" *(Psalm 103:13–14).*

Verse 12 of this psalm speaks of God removing our sins "as far as the east is from the west." This doesn't mean we should treat our sins lightly, but when we sin, we don't have to be afraid to tell God we're sorry. He "is faithful and just and will forgive us our sins and purify us from all unrighteousness" (1 John 1:9). By his Spirit within us, he can help us improve our behavior.

In the Book of Romans, Paul talks about the old system and the new system. In the old system, people were slaves to the law. When they broke God's law, they feared God's punishment. But in the new system, we have been adopted as God's children. We are in the family, and God treats us as his own. "For you did not receive a spirit that makes you a slave again to fear, but you received the Spirit of adoption. And by this Spirit, we can call God 'Daddy'!" (Romans 8:15, my translation).

So if you feel like a slave to fear, cowering in terror before an angry God, break out of those chains. Enjoy a loving, tender relationship with your heavenly Father.

MEMORY VERSE

Psalm 103:13
As a father has compassion on his children, so the Lord has compassion on those who fear him.

This psalm is full of wonderful expressions of praise to God and expressions of God's love for us. A psalm like this disproves the idea that the New Testament deals with God's grace and love while the Old Testament contains only laws and judgment. The reference to "dust" in verse 14 refers to the creation, when God made Adam from the dust of the earth.

1. Check off the times below when you need to remember this passage.

☐ When you've just made a major mistake

☐ When you're afraid that God may not love you anymore

☐ When you think God's standards are impossible to meet

☐ When you think other Christians have it all figured out, but you don't

☐ Other ____

2. Rephrase verse 13 for someone who has not had a loving earthly father.

____

3. Our faith is based on an understanding that God is holy, and demands holiness. What does Psalm 103 show us about God's feelings toward us?

____

4. Picture yourself standing before God's throne saying, "I'm sorry for my sin." Based on this psalm and other scriptures, how do you think God would respond to you? What would he say?

____

☐ I have read the material on facing down the unhealthy fear of God on pages 53–54, which introduces this week's Adventure theme.

☐ I have prayed the Facing Down Our Fears Prayer (see p. 8).

☐ I have started memorizing Psalm 103:13.

☐ I've done the outrageously courageous act preparation exercises (pp. 48–49).

Read Luke 15:11–32.

1. What TV show might use this story as the framework for a plot line? Which TV characters would play which biblical characters?

____

____

2. Which character in this story do you most identify with—father, younger brother, older brother, or maybe the pigs? Why?

____

____

3. If the younger son could have written the script for this story—and it sounds like he started to do so—what kind of welcome-home response would he expect from his father?

____

____

4. Why do you think the father welcomed back the younger son?

____

5. It's pretty clear that the father represents God in this story. With that in mind, does this story affect your image of God? If so, how?

____

____

☐ I have read the material on facing down the unhealthy fear of God on pages 53–54, which introduces this week's Adventure theme.

☐ I have prayed today using the Facing Down Our Fears Prayer (see p. 8).

☐ I am memorizing Psalm 103:13.

☐ I have been a Barnabas for two people and recorded my progress on page 10.

☐ I have done the outrageously courageous act preparation exercises on pages 48–49.

☐ I am planning a Discussion Time with family or friends to talk about the unhealthy fear of God (see p. 12).

Read Micah 7:18–20.

Micah's name means, "Who is like the Lord?" The first line in verse 18 is a play on words using his name. Micah prophesied during a time of ups and downs for the people of Judah. Micah's message is twofold, warning of God's judgment on sin, but also promising redemption.

1. Some people think God is usually angry and vengeful. Do you know anyone like this? If so, how would you describe his or her attitude?

____

____

2. How is God described in these verses?

____

____

3. Advertisements regularly use the same pattern found in this passage. They start with, "What else is like our product?" and then they trumpet its virtues. Using the descriptions of God from this text, write a 15-second radio commercial praising the unique qualities of God.

____

____

____

4. Do you have a hard time believing God will forgive certain sins you've committed? If so, talk with God about those sins. God longs to forgive you, if you'll let him. Tell him just how you feel.

- [ ] I have prayed today using the Facing Down Our Fears Prayer (see p. 8).
- [ ] I am memorizing Psalm 103:13.
- [ ] I have decided on a third person to encourage and have noted that on page 10.
- [ ] I have done the outrageously courageous act preparation exercises on pages 48–49.
- [ ] I am planning a Discussion Time with family or friends to talk about the unhealthy fear of God (see p. 12).

Read Isaiah 49:13–16a.

1. How can mountains "burst into song"?

____

2. Write four lines of a love song that God might sing to his people, based on this passage.

____

____

____

____

3. Do you ever feel that the Lord has "forsaken" or "forgotten" you? How would this passage affect you at such times?

____

____

4. What other comparison might you use to demonstrate God's compassion to someone who has not had a loving relationship with his or her mother?

____

____

5. "I have engraved you on the palms of my hands" is the sort of stark image you might expect from the Violent Femmes or Crash Test Dummies. What do you think it means? How would you express it in another way?

____

____

☐ I have prayed today using the Facing Down Our Fears Prayer (see p. 8).

☐ I am memorizing Psalm 103:13.

☐ I have decided on a third person to encourage and have noted that on page 10.

☐ I have completed my outrageously courageous act and have evaluated my effort on page 49.

☐ I am planning a Discussion Time with family or friends to talk about the unhealthy fear of God (see p. 12).

Read Zephaniah 3:14–17.

Zephaniah, who lived about the same time as Jeremiah, also foretold the destruction of Jerusalem by the Babylonians. Zephaniah also hints at the eventual return of Israel to Jerusalem. Sure enough, after 70 years in captivity, the Israelites were allowed to return to their homeland.

1. According to Zephaniah, what has God already done?

____

____

2. What is he still planning to do?

____

____

3. What do you think is the significance of letting your hands "hang limp"?

____

____

4. What could you do with your hands instead that would celebrate the Lord's presence?

____

____

☐ I have prayed today using the Facing Down Our Fears Prayer (see p. 8).

☐ I am memorizing Psalm 103:13.

☐ I have been a Barnabas for three people and recorded my progress on page 10.

☐ I have completed my outrageously courageous act and have evaluated my effort on page 49.

☐ I have scheduled a Discussion Time with family or friends to talk about the unhealthy fear of God (see p. 12).

Read Proverbs 9:10.

1. Based on the Bible readings this week, do you think you ought to be afraid of God? If not, how would you define "the fear of the Lord" in today's verse?

____

2. In Hebrew poetry the second line is often a restatement of the first. In that case, the fear of the Lord would be equated with "the knowledge of the Holy One." How might that affect your definition?

____

3. According to Proverbs 16:6, what is one result of fearing God?

____

4. If someone is terrified to think about or approach God, that's an *unhealthy* fear of the Lord. But giving God the reverence and respect he deserves is a healthy fear of the Lord. How do you think a *healthy* fear of God would be demonstrated in a person's life?

☐ Eating nutritious broccoli and saying grace over it

    ☐ Putting a dust cover on your Bible

☐ Singing majestic hymns of the faith, but adding a reggae beat

    ☐ Committing any sin you want, but feeling guilty about it

☐ Other (And I'm hoping *you* have some better ideas for this one.)

    ☐ _______________________________________

☐ _______________________________________

☐ I have prayed today using the Facing Down Our Fears Prayer (see p. 8).

☐ I have memorized Psalm 103:13 and recorded my progress on page 6.

☐ I have read *How to Fear God Without Being Afraid of Him* and scheduled a Discussion Time with family or friends to talk about the unhealthy fear of God (see p. 12).

    ☐ I have been a Barnabas for three people and recorded my progress on page 10.

    ☐ I have completed my outrageously courageous act and have evaluated my effort on page 49.

Growing Up, Breaking Down

This week we're facing down the fear of sickness, aging, and death. To be honest, your parents and grandparents probably deal with these fears a lot more than you do. But even at your age, certain worries can creep into your life.

The fear of a permanent or recurring sickness or injury. If someone close to you, especially someone your age, suddenly becomes sick or injured, it can be a major jolt. You have expectations of good health, right? You look forward to the freedom to do whatever you want to as a healthy adult. But what if that freedom is cut short by some physical problem?

The fear of a disaster that brings death or injury. You've heard the news stories—a car full of kids coming home from a school dance gets blindsided by a drunk driver. It happens too often—young people's lives cut short. You think of all the things you haven't done yet. Could an accident like that happen to you?

The fear of your parents or grandparents growing old. You may be seeing this already. Grandma doesn't see as well. Grandpa doesn't remember things. Dad gets tired climbing steps. You may be too young to worry about your own aging, but you see the results in others, and it bothers you.

Sickness, aging, and death are grim realities in this world. They remind us that our earthly lives are not everything. The process of decay and dying is a natural part of our world, but we look forward to a kingdom where those processes are nonexistent. In the presence of God we have eternal life.

In the famous Twenty-third Psalm (our memory verse for this week), David spoke of the fear of death.

"Even though I walk through the valley of the shadow of death, I will fear no evil, for you are with me" (Psalm 23:4).

The specter of death may be among us, but even physical death is not "evil" in God's presence. For people who know God, death is only a graduation into a much better life.

Sickness and physical limitations are hard to endure, but God can provide all the strength we need to bear these things. When we are physically weak, God's power comes through for us. As he told Paul, who was suffering with some kind of ailment, "My power is made perfect in weakness" (2 Corinthians 12:9).

It is natural to be sad about sickness and death. Even Jesus wept at Lazarus' tomb. But we do not need to fear these things, as long as we live in the presence of God.

MEMORY VERSE

Psalm 23:4
Even though I walk through the valley of the shadow of death, I will fear no evil, for you are with me; your rod and your staff, they comfort me.

This familiar psalm uses the image of God as a shepherd. David was a shepherd himself, and so he knew the responsibilities involved—protecting, guiding, providing for the flock, and so on. The shepherd's rod was generally used to club down any wild animals that might attack. The staff nudged the sheep in the right direction. The valley of the shadow of death could have been, literally, a dark, dangerous valley through which sheep were herded. But it also can represent the fearful times we all face.

1. Check off any of the situations you might face this week when you need to remember this verse.

☐ When you are seriously tempted

☐ When you fear for your safety

☐ When you worry about dying

☐ When you think God must be far away

☐ When no one else seems to care about God anymore

☐ Other _______________________________________

☐ _______________________________________

2. You're hired to do a dramatic reading of Psalm 23 on MTV, but the executive vice president wants some changes. "Where do you see shepherds anymore? That's old hat, history, been-there-done-that, stale as yesterday's guacamole. Give me a new image, baby, something for today, something that speaks my language." How would you translate the message of Psalm 23 into more up-to-date imagery?

____
____
____
____
____
____

3. More seriously, now, is there a place, a time, a group of people, or a specific situation in your life that you might classify as a sort of "valley of the shadow of death"? Explain.

____

____

4. What's it like there? Choose five words that might describe the experience of walking through that symbolic "valley."

A 3-letter word _______________

A 4-letter word (not that kind!) _________

A 5-letter word _______________

A 6-letter word _______________

A 7-letter word _______________

5. How does it help you to know that the Lord is always with you during those times?

____

____

☐ I have read the material on facing down the fear of sickness, aging, and death on page 61, which introduces this week's Adventure theme.

☐ I have prayed today using the Facing Down Our Fears Prayer (see p. 8).

☐ I have started memorizing Psalm 23:4.

☐ I have scheduled a Discussion Time with family or friends.

"FIRST OF ALL DAD, A LAWN MOWER SPEWS ALL KINDS OF TOXINS INTO THE AIR AND DEPLETES THE OZONE LAYER. SECONDLY, GRASS GIVES OFF OXYGEN AND BY CUTTING IT WE LITERALLY CHOKE EVERY LIVING CREATURE. BUT, IF THAT'S WHAT YOU WANT ME TO DO, DAD, I'LL DO IT."

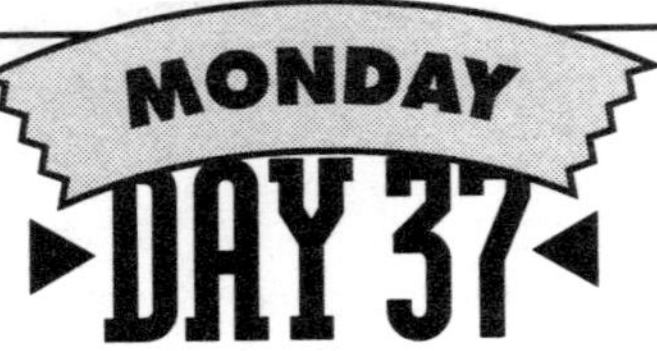

Read Lamentations 3:19–26.

The Book of Lamentations describes how Jerusalem was destroyed by the Babylonians. It's a heartbreaking and depressing book, yet in the middle of it, the author (possibly Jeremiah) sounds a note of hope.

1. Other than death, what do you think is the worst thing that can happen to someone your age?

____

2. Suppose you're a counselor on a call-in radio show and a person calls with the problem you just described. Based on today's reading, what advice or assurance would you give this person?

____

3. How does someone "seek" God? (verse 25)

____

4. This week your Adventure focuses on the fear of sickness, aging, and death. You're probably not too concerned about aging, but sickness and even death may be grim realities to you. You may also be worried about your future. Will you be able to make a good living, to get a good job, to buy a house of your own, to get married and establish a good relationship?

How difficult is it for you to "wait for God"? Some people are naturally patient; what about you? On a scale of 7 to 23, how difficult is it for you to "wait" without worrying about these things? (23 is most difficult) _______

5. How does this message of God's faithfulness help calm your fears?

____

6. Take some time now to talk with God about these issues. Ask him to help you develop and maintain hope.

☐ I have read the material on facing down the fear of sickness, aging, and death on page 61, which introduces this week's Adventure theme.

☐ I have prayed the Facing Down Our Fears Prayer (see p. 8).

☐ I am memorizing Psalm 23:4.

☐ I have scheduled a Discussion Time with family or friends.

Read 2 Corinthians 12:7–10.

1. Based on Paul's description of his "thorn in the flesh," what do you think it might have been?

- [ ] A recurring disease of some kind
- [ ] Some coworker Paul didn't like
- [ ] An actual thorn he couldn't remove
- [ ] Some addiction or ongoing struggle with sin
- [ ] Other ____
- [ ] Blindness
- [ ] Paul's wife

Actually, most of the previous options have been suggested by Bible scholars, but we just don't know for sure. What's important is that there was some kind of problem that Paul wanted God to remove, and God wouldn't.

2. Why do you think God allowed Paul to struggle with an ongoing problem?

____

3. Some people suggest that any sickness or struggle is an indication that God is punishing the person for something, or that the person must be out of the will of God. After reading this passage, would you agree or disagree with this point of view? Why?

____

4. Do you know any Christians who are physically weak, yet have great spiritual strength? What can you learn from such people?

____

5. You may be struggling with certain "thorns" yourself, things that make you feel out of place in a world that prizes perfection. You may consider yourself too fat, too pimply, too dumb, or whatever. How can this passage improve your attitude toward your own problems or weaknesses?

____

- [ ] I have prayed the Facing Down Our Fears Prayer (see p. 8).
- [ ] I am memorizing Psalm 23:4.
- [ ] I have scheduled a Discussion Time with family or friends to talk about the unhealthy fear of God (see p. 12).

Read Psalm 92:12–15.

1. This psalm uses the images of the palm tree and the cedar tree to represent righteous people. See if you can find another way to symbolize righteous people. Look around and try to use a symbol from your area.

"The righteous will flourish like ____"

2. What do you think the earth will be like in 50 years (if it's around at all)?

☐ Blown to smithereens
☐ A polluted garbage dump
☐ Everything run by technology
☐ A lush jungle
☐ Pretty much like it is now
☐ Other ________________________

☐ A post-nuclear wasteland
☐ Cold, steel buildings everywhere
☐ Peaceful and harmonious
☐ A scientific utopia
☐ Jesus will return by then

3. Think about yourself at age 80. Which of the following do you expect will describe you at that point?

☐ Like Kramer on "Seinfeld"
☐ Caring for others
☐ Praising God
☐ Wise

☐ Still youthful and good-looking
☐ Self-centered
☐ Depressed
☐ Other ________________________

4. What promises in today's verses might reassure you as you look toward the future?

____

5. Though you may not be worried about aging, your parents might be. What kind of encouragement could you give them, or to others who might be concerned about growing older?

____

☐ I have prayed the Facing Down Our Fears Prayer (see p. 8).
☐ I am memorizing Psalm 23:4.
☐ I have discussed the unhealthy fear of God with family or friends.

Read John 11:17–27.

1. Have you ever had a close call, maybe you were nearly in a car accident, or there was a shooting in a place where you had recently been? How do you feel when such things take place?

____

2. What does today's text say about Jesus' power over life and death?

____

3. Lazarus isn't still hanging around Bethany. Jesus didn't mean that his followers would never die physically. So what *was* he promising?

____

Jesus often used his physical miracles as evidence of his spiritual power. When a paralyzed man was brought to him, Jesus declared his sins forgiven (Mark 2:1–12). This caused problems for the religious leaders who knew that only God had power to forgive sins. So Jesus asked, "Which is easier: to say to the paralytic, 'Your sins are forgiven' or to say, 'Get up, take your mat and walk'?"

Of course, it's easier to *say*, "Your sins are forgiven," because no one can test it out. But if you say that a paralyzed man is healed and he still can't walk, your opponents can prove you're a fraud.

So Jesus did what everyone thought was harder. He turned and told the paralyzed man to get up and walk. And he did. The physical healing was a *sign* of Jesus' even more important ability to heal us spiritually.

4. How did this minisermon affect your attitude toward death?

☐ It still stinks (death, that is, not the sermon)

   ☐ When you gotta go, it's nice to have somewhere to go to

☐ I can't wait!

   ☐ I can wait about another 90 years

☐ I still have some uncertainties about death

   ☐ Other _______________________________

☐ I have prayed the Facing Down Our Fears Prayer (see p. 8).

☐ I am memorizing Psalm 23:4.

☐ I have discussed the unhealthy fear of God with family or friends.

Read Luke 2:21-38.

1. What was Simeon waiting for?

____

2. What do you suppose a day in Simeon's life would be like?

____

3. How do you think Simeon felt when he saw the baby Jesus?

____

4. What seemed to be Anna's priority in life?

____

5. On an excitement scale of 1 to 10 (10 being the most), how would you rate the lives of Simeon and Anna? _____
On the same scale, rate the level of excitement in your own life. _____

I want to zero in on a fear that I'll call the fear of missing out. Many kids get into drug and alcohol abuse, sexual involvements, vandalism, and other problems because they're afraid they'll miss out on something. Others live in almost continual dejection, worrying that life is somehow passing them by.

6. What things do you suppose Simeon and Anna "missed out on" while they spent so much time in the temple?

____

Now think about what they _didn't_ miss—Jesus. They had their priorities straight. They were ready when the Savior of the world came to town.

7. Do you have a fear of missing out? What are some questionable things you're frequently tempted to take part in? How could a priority adjustment help you find more satisfaction while you're missing out on those activities?

____

☐ I have prayed the Facing Down Our Fears Prayer (see p. 8).

☐ I have memorized Psalm 23:4 and recorded my progress on page 6.

☐ I have read _How to Fear God Without Being Afraid of Him._

☐ I have been a Barnabas for three people and recorded my progress on page 10.

All in the Family

Josh and Steve were good kids. Sure, they were adventurous teenagers who sometimes got into trouble, but they were sweet-spirited. I liked them a lot. Their parents were strong Christians, anchors in their church. The family seemed to be the model for a healthy Christian family.

But then Mom and Dad started having problems. They eventually separated, then divorced. Josh and Steve moved back and forth between their parents. When finances became a problem, Josh had to get a job and forget about college. Then Mom lost her job and had to sell the house, so they were uprooted again.

All of this took a toll on the two boys. Steve grew sullen; Josh got apathetic. Their joyous personalities were damaged by these events over which they had no control.

This week we're focusing on the fear of threats to our families. I don't want to scare you, but in today's world, family life can be shaky. Divorce is splitting up many families. Unemployment can drain a family's savings in no time. In our highly mobile society, frequent moves can take their toll on family stability.

In some fearful situations, you can do certain things, but others you have no control over. A famous prayer says, "God grant me the serenity to accept the things I cannot change, the courage to change the things I can, and the wisdom to know the difference." That makes a lot of sense.

In the case of Josh and Steve, they had no control over the bad things that were happening, and that caused them pain. But they also made decisions about how to respond to the situation, and I believe they made some bad choices. They may have blamed themselves for all the bad developments and got so depressed they couldn't think straight.

One thing that you can be sure of, even if everything else falls apart, is God's love. Even if the people nearest and dearest to you suddenly let you down, God will *never* leave you. As our memory verse for this week says,

"But from everlasting to everlasting the Lord's love is with those who fear him" (Psalm 103:17).

Be sure to remember that "those who fear him" means "those who *honor him*," or "those who *care about how God feels.*"

Things may happen to your family that you can't control. If your parents split up, or if Mom loses her job, don't blame yourself. Instead, you can help pick up the pieces by deciding to live in a way that honors God.

►DAYS 42-43◄

MEMORY VERSE

Psalm 103:17
But from everlasting to everlasting the Lord's love is with those who fear him, and his righteousness with their children's children.

We've been in Psalm 103 before (see days 28/29). The verses just before verse 17 talk about how *temporary* humanity is. In contrast, God's love is eternal.

1. Check off any of the situations you expect to face this week when you think you might need to remember this verse.

- [ ] When you think you don't deserve God's love
- [ ] When you feel lonely
- [ ] When you feel as if no one loves you
- [ ] When you want to celebrate God's love
- [ ] When you wonder if good times are going to last
- [ ] Other ______________________________________

2. What do you think the word *fear* means in this verse?

____

3. Rewrite Psalm 103:17 without using the words *love* or *fear*.

____

4. This verse goes on to describe God's blessings on families. "His righteousness" is even with the grandchildren of those who fear him. Do you have a "spiritual heritage"? Have your parents or grandparents taught you to love the Lord? Or are you starting a relationship with God by yourself? Explain.

____

5. How have your parents or grandparents affected your relationship with God?

____

6. Take some time to pray for your family members.

- [ ] I have read the material on facing down the fear of threats to our families on page 69, which introduces this week's Adventure theme.
- [ ] I have prayed the Facing Down Our Fears Prayer (see p. 8).
- [ ] I have started memorizing Psalm 103:17.

Read Matthew 21:14–16.

Many kids have fears about their families—that their parents will split up, or lose their jobs, or have to move. Others struggle with disease in their families, or worry about the death of their parents or grandparents. We're going to try to zero in on *your* role in such circumstances. How can you honor God even in an uncertain family situation?

1. In today's text, what were the "young people" doing?

____

____

2. What was Jesus' response to the authorities?

____

____

3. Have you ever been restricted by some authority when you were trying to do something good? When?

____

____

4. Have you ever felt that you were being put down because of your age—that adults didn't pay attention to you because you were just a kid? Explain.

____

____

5. What encouragement does today's text provide for such situations?

____

6. You can play a key role in your family's spiritual life. You can be a source of spiritual strength. What's one thing you could do to make a difference in your family's relationship with God?

____

- [ ] I have read the material on facing down the fear of threats to our families on page 69, which introduces this week's Adventure theme.
- [ ] I have prayed the Facing Down Our Fears Prayer (see p. 8).
- [ ] I am memorizing Psalm 103:17.

Read Ephesians 6:1–9.

1. According to this text, what are your responsibilities in your home?

____

____

2. How well do you think you do in this department? Give yourself a letter grade (A to F). _______

3. What are the responsibilities of your parents ("fathers" in the verse)?

____

____

4. How well do you think your parents do in this department?
    Father's Grade: _______
    Mother's Grade: _______

5. Which of the statements in this passage do you think would have been most surprising to the people in Ephesus who first read it?

____

____

6. I think the key to this passage is *relationship*. Family is a two-way street (or a multilane highway). Each member is responsible for treating everyone else with honor, respect, and love. That means that you can lovingly ask to be treated with more respect—especially if you're feeling "exasperated." In return, you must do more than obey—you must "honor" your parents. What do you think is the difference between honoring and merely obeying?

____

____

7. What is one thing you could do to improve a relationship within your family?

____

____

☐ I have prayed today using the Facing Down Our Fears Prayer (see p. 8).
☐ I am memorizing Psalm 103:17.

Read 2 Timothy 3:14–17.

Paul wrote this letter to the young minister Timothy. The first part of chapter 3 details the problems in society that would occur "in the last days." These problems were beginning to happen back then, and they're more evident now.

1. In verses 14–17, what does Paul want Timothy to do?

____

____

2. What does 2 Timothy 1:5 tell you about Timothy's childhood?

____

____

3. How does the Bible affect the development of a believer?

☐ Teaching truth

    ☐ Adding color to a dingy coffee table

☐ Showing where we need to shape up

    ☐ Giving us something to quote to sound holy

☐ Sharing practical advice for living

    ☐ Offering a place to jot key phone numbers

☐ Other _______________________________

A "family" doesn't have to be Mom, Dad, 2.4 kids, and the dog. The New Testament emphasizes that the *church* is a family. If your family is not Christian, you may need to find a caring group of Christians to be a spiritual family for you.

You may have fears about your family's future or be worried about family members. But God can continue to help you grow, and he can use *you* to strengthen family relationships.

☐ I have prayed the Facing Down Our Fears Prayer (see p. 8).

☐ I have memorized Psalm 103:17 and recorded my progress on page 6.

☐ I have read *How to Fear God Without Being Afraid of Him*.

The Rise and Fall of the Evil Empire

When I was in college, I helped lead a youth group at a nearby church. As we planned the Bible studies, we asked the kids what part of the Bible they were most interested in. The answer was unanimous: the Book of Revelation.

This was not a book I wanted to deal with. There are so many different opinions about this book, it seems impossible to understand it. What's Babylon? Who's the beast? What role does the European Common Market play in the end times? Will Red China send an army across the Euphrates? When will the bowls of wrath be poured out? Which option is correct: premillennial, midtribulational, or postnasal drip?

Some scholars and authors think they have all the details of this complex book worked out. Books and movies present various interpretations in great detail. Often, they scare people. In fact, I think that's why my youth group wanted to study Revelation. It's weird, it's a challenge, and much of it is frightening. It's like watching *Nightmare on Church Street*.

Years later, with a different group, I finally did lead a study of Revelation. And I found the often-missed secret to the book. Are you ready? Here it is, *the* key to Revelation, the answer you've all been waiting for, the essential element for understanding the end times.

God wins.

Do not get confused about the fields of Armageddon. Do not be perplexed about who or what the antichrist is. Read right through and you'll find the most glorious victory of all time. Jesus Christ defeats the forces of evil. Good Friday was D-day, and the Resurrection assured that God had won the battle. The rest of history is a mop-up operation.

Today you'll find a lot of Christians who get very alarmed about the rise of evil in the world. They point to social trends, political decisions, wars and rumors of wars, and even start comparing them with details in Revelation or Daniel. But don't ever forget that crucial point: God wins.

Our memory verse makes it personal:

"But the Lord is faithful, and he will strengthen and protect you from the evil one" (2 Thessalonians 3:3).

Whenever evil seems to be surrounding you, and when you feel strongly tempted, you do not need to be afraid. The forces of evil are the losing team in the struggle of the ages. You can rely on the Lord's power for protection, because . . . (all together now!) . . . God wins!

Read John 17:13–19.

1. Have you ever been in a situation where you felt out of place? Exactly how did you feel?

____

The word *world* in the Gospel of John refers to the whole range of human values and desires that are opposed to God. If you're "of the world," you share its values and feel comfortable with its ways. Jesus was challenging his followers to live according to a new and better system.

2. Let's have some fun with this:

Of the World: Look out for "number one"
Not of the World: Turn "fractional" people into "whole numbers"
Of the World: Make as much dough as you can
Not of the World: Buy free pizza for everybody

Get it? Dough? Pizza? Fill in the next few comparisons with statements that are clever, funny, or maybe even true.

Of the World: Party hearty until you can't see straight
Not of the World: _______________________________

Not of the World: Do to others as you would like them to do to you.
Of the World: _______________________________

And try one on your own:

Of the World: _______________________________
Not of the World: _______________________________

3. What did Jesus pray for his disciples in verse 15? Why?

____

4. How do you think God's truth "sanctifies" us ("sets us apart")?

____

☐ I have read the material on facing down the fear of the rise of evil on page 74, which introduces this week's Adventure theme.

☐ I have prayed the Facing Down Our Fears Prayer (see p. 8).

☐ I have started memorizing 2 Thessalonians 3:3.

▶DAY 48◀

Read Colossians 2:13–15.

In the ancient world, a victorious general would return from battle and parade through the streets of the city with his army. He would also march the defeated army through the city, disarmed and humiliated, as a "public spectacle." Paul uses this image to describe Christ's triumph over evil.

1. List God's actions that are mentioned in this passage.

____

2. What are the regulations he has "canceled out"?

____

3. How do you usually feel when you see evil—people acting as if God does not exist or does not matter, and even taking advantage of good people?

____

____

4. After reading a passage like this, do your feelings about evil change at all? If so, how?

____

____

☐ I have read the material on facing down the fear of the rise of evil on page 74, which introduces this week's Adventure theme.

☐ I have prayed today using the Facing Down Our Fears Prayer (see p. 8).

☐ I have started memorizing 2 Thessalonians 3:3.

MEMORY VERSE

2 Thessalonians 3:3
But the Lord is faithful, and he will strengthen and protect you from the evil one.

here's a short Greek lesson for you. In the original Greek, the word translated "is" in this verse has a special meaning. It refers not only to who God is, it also includes what he *does*. So he is not just a faithful God. He is actively being faithful. It's a hands-on activity.

Paul, the author of this letter, is facing opposition to his faith and is very aware of God's faithfulness. In the previous verses he asked for prayer. He assured them that the Lord would continue doing faithful things, despite the evil forces all around them.

1. Check off the times below when you most need to remember this verse.

☐ When you're being tempted to do wrong

☐ When people make fun of you for being a Christian

☐ When you're frustrated by the evil in society

☐ When you wonder whether God knows what's going on down here

☐ Other ____

☐ ____

2. In verse 2, Paul asks for deliverance from "wicked and evil men." What kind of dangers do you suppose he faced? (See 2 Corinthians 11:23–28 for some clues.)

____

____

____

3. What dangers do *you* face from "wicked and evil people"?

____

____

____

4. The Thessalonians were very interested in the end times. In both his letters to them, Paul told them what to expect. The rise of evil in society was clearly one sign to watch for. Yet some Christians today seem to be fearful about the events prophesied for the end times. Do you know any people like this? How could you use a passage like this (that focuses on the faithfulness of God) to comfort such a person?

____

____

____

5. As you confront people who act in evil ways, or face systems that promote evil, what can you do to resist them?

- [ ] Pray a lot
    - [ ] Tell evil people how wrong they are
- [ ] Warn people about hell
    - [ ] Turn the other cheek, whatever that means
- [ ] Keep telling people about the love of Jesus
    - [ ] Depend on God's power
- [ ] Form your fingers in the shape of a cross and shout, "Back, you nasty person"

- [ ] I have prayed today using the Facing Down Our Fears Prayer (see p. 8).
- [ ] I am memorizing 2 Thessalonians 3:3.

Read 1 Peter 1:3–5.

1. Have you known about a special treat—some great gift or experience—awaiting you in the future but you had to wait? What was it?

2. How did you feel while you were waiting for it?

3. Today's text describes an inheritance waiting for us, an exciting eternal life with God and all the privileges that go with it. How do you feel about waiting for such a gift?

4. What has the resurrection of Jesus Christ accomplished, according to these verses?

5. This passage has past, present, and future aspects to it—though some are more obvious than others. Dig a little and jot down what you find.

In the Past
*
*
*

In the Present
*
*
*

In the Future
*
*
*

6. What do you think God's power "shields" us from?

7. Have you ever felt "shielded" by God? In what ways?

____

____

8. As we see the power of evil in society, we don't need to be afraid. By his resurrection, Jesus Christ proved that he had power over the forces of evil. And we're on his side. What can you do today to celebrate the resurrection of Jesus Christ?

____

____

☐ I have prayed today using the Facing Down Our Fears Prayer (see p. 8).

☐ I have memorized 2 Thessalonians 3:3 and recorded my progress on page 6.

☐ I have read *How to Fear God Without Being Afraid of Him*.

☐ I have been a Barnabas for three people and recorded my progress on page 10.

☐ I have completed my outrageously courageous act and have evaluated my effort on page 49.

☐ I have discussed the unhealthy fear of God with family or friends.

The Chapel Ministries appreciates any comments you have about this year's Adventure. Write to us at:

**The Chapel Ministries
Editorial Department
Box 30
Wheaton, IL 60189**